NOBODY
OWNS THE WORLD

A simple manual to using your
common sense again,

Author Mr. Nobody

once you recognize me, you see yourself

Nobody wants to take the first step!

Do you want to be kept informed about new
developments, local social media events or when the
next booklet comes out?

The title of my next booklet is promising:
Nobody is Sovereign with the subtitle,
How to: Start a Project
Leave your name and
email:
mrnobodyibiza@proton.me

INDEX

Illustrations explained

INTRODUCTION

Dear Beautiful Soul,

First, I want to get something clear as I don't have all the answers. When I use the word 'truth' in this booklet I actually mean to say; this is no lie. Using the word truth is easier for all to read. I hope you'll forgive me for that. Now let's get straight to the point, sometimes when I look around, I wonder, *'What kind of world do we actually live in; is this really our choice or is it meant to be; and, if it is meant to be, by whom, and why?'* All questions that you have, you will get answers or insights about after reading my booklet.

Definitions Page. I want to point out that some of the terminology used in my booklet will be new to you, therefore I've created a Definitions Page in the backend of this booklet for you to refer to when you might be confused on some of the terms.

But before I tell my story, dear reader, let me thank you for being brave enough to read this. It will question your beliefs and thus make you look at yourself differently. Well, to the better version of yourself, which is my intention. The booklet is therefore intended to make you aware as a human being and thus to help you better understand what is happening around you. How you can keep up with it, or even better, enjoy it. Of course, it would be great if this booklet was used as a basis for real conversations with loved ones, friends, or family about these important but sensitive topics.

Most people in our society have no idea what is actually happening in society behind the scenes and what they are really working on, let alone whether, and how they can possibly get out of this. For all unconscious and conscious people, but also for people who are related with secret societies and for those who have no idea about it, I thought it would be a great idea to write this booklet. The information I reveal to you will provide everyone with equal opportunities in living in this society.

How? I will reveal occult secrets, this literally means hidden secrets and by share generally unknown knowledge. This is a good start to take the invisible powers away from that which controls us; I will shine a little light in the darkness you might say.

In this booklet I use strong words, such as satanism, black magic and occult. Not to scare you, but to make you aware that they exist and so that I am able to better explain the world where we live in. So don't react shocked but allow yourself to look at it with an open mind. Let it come to you as a human being who is here to experience his free will and to learn from each other.

I will explain this as clearly as possible, in short chapters that don't lie, supplemented with useful facts and quotes that tell you something.

My main character in the booklet is called 'Nobody'.

Nobody is somebody who reminds you of simple things you may have forgotten or gives you a different perspective on what you already know. Nobody shares facts worth knowing and uses them to make connections that were unknown for a long time, and therefore invisible to you and me.
If these words are new and inspire you, it could be the beginning of your journey to unravelling the real

secret about your very own existence. When you begin to understand the dynamics, this is when you will begin to take back the control of your very existence. If the ride feels a little bumpy along the way, keep reading, and remember …

It's a beautiful love story…

CHAPTER ONE

TO BE SOMEONE
The role-play

The game of life. Everybody wants to mean something in it. You want to mean something to others, or perhaps to the entire world. Those are good intentions. But to mean something to others, *you have to be someone*. That 'someone' is usually not who you really are, but a role you play that serves a function to get you somewhere or realise something. A role that you saw in others and have also taught yourself. If you play it well, your role will mean something to others.

We play many roles without even realising it. What most do not think about is that you can play roles that benefit your financial career, but you can also spend time to play roles that enrich your social career. In the latter case, the roles do not have anything to do with money or work, but have everything to do with friendship or family or even with passion and love. If you play many roles, it can sometimes be difficult to do everything right. For example, as a juggler trying to keep too many balls in the air, if he loses control, it looks funny and if the balls fall, the show is over.

Now imagine you are playing all your roles perfectly; your show went on and you became very successful and everything in your business career worked out. Then at some point in your life you are there with all your money and possessions, probably somewhere in the sun, enjoying a nice drink. Then, if you are brave enough and still dare to look outside your own comfort zone, you will be reminded that your wealth does not bring real pleasure or happiness, because then you see that the world is dying of hunger, and more clear our earth is in her worst conditions; nothing good for the children of this world.

This is a result of your wealth and is what you might call the flip side of success. Everything around you is based on money and is bought, not earned, including mostly fake friends, fake girlfriends and so on. They bring you everything but give you nothing. In other words, money does not make you rich, it is the real experiences that make you rich as a human being. In a successful existence where many want something from you or with you, because of your wealth or for who you are, an authentic experience is hard to find.

Our main character, Nobody is "someone" who realises that time is your best friend and also that time is our most precious gift in this life. And because of this realisation, Nobody stops wasting time on things that don't make sense anymore. By learning to feel what feels good, to accept the situation as it is and then act from love for yourself and live your life.

From one perspective I could state that, everything is energy. Every object, seen or unseen is *energy*, energy that is expressing its different manners to our perspective. Using a microscope, I will prove this statement. So, to create a frame of reference that we can relate to, I am speaking about our divine existence as human beings, living together here on earth as humanity, full of intentionally created chaos that we are part of as a victim or as the audience as opposed to where we are from, our 'real' world.

As a human being, we all have a brain and therefore, the power to create. The placebo effect shows how powerful our brain really is. Our brain is made up of two spheres. Simply put, a creative part that can come up with ideas and a logical part that can explain or bring it into action. These sometimes-abstract ideas, we call concepts.

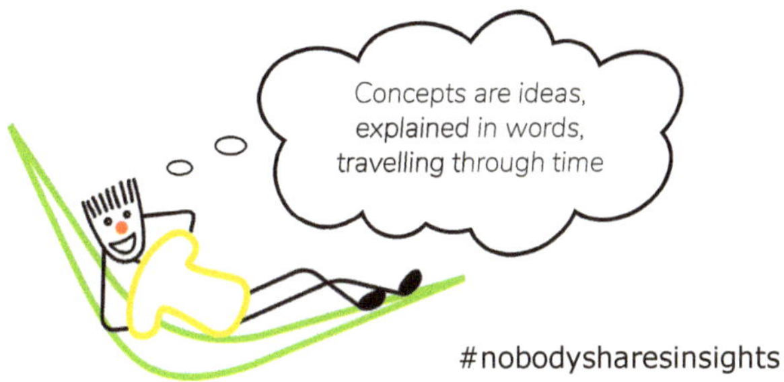

One can say, 'human' is also just an idea, or a concept, to go deeper in the meaning of this phrase I need a separate booklet. That would be too much for now.

Let's get back to the abstract ideas that we call concepts. We as humans can use these concepts to explain something. But what we explain is not 'really' true since a concept is just an idea. That is why the truth has different perceptions of the same truth.

To give you an example, there is a concept that explains that our soul has chosen this experience here on Earth. And that we, the people who experience a soul in our bodies, are here for a reason. If you look at it that way, it explains answers to questions people get, when they think a little deeper about themselves or about life. After all, we are all looking for the truth somewhere, or at least "our" truth.

We have also been taught to believe or even worship something or someone greater or higher than ourselves. In addition to seeing our parents as leaders, we can also look up to a teacher at school, a successful businessperson, a pop star, a great therapist, coach, or even spiritual leader … it's all a distraction. By believing them, you give your power away and stop questioning yourself about who you are, and what you came to Earth to learn. You will have all kinds of experiences during your life that you can see as lessons. Your beliefs, which is what you believe in now, will be questioned by situations in life and this will test your world view.

If you can see your life as I described, consciously or unconsciously, you are on a path in search for the truth. That process is called becoming aware. Most people are unaware and going through life living in society not asking questions. You become aware of the fact that material things or outside influences do not provide real happiness.
Everything is within.

Using questions of self-reflection can help this process to better understand, what keeps you away from your happiness, then solving that and thereby becoming increasingly aware of who you truly are, what your passions are or even what your purpose is, in this life. That was deep.
Now breath pause and integrate… Well done.

Let's get back to the story about Nobody.

CHAPTER TWO

From Somebody to Nobody

Where do I come from?

Let me tell you how it happened that somebody became a 'Nobody' and what Nobody had to do to lose it; that is, to experience everything for a period, like a nobody, to live outside the box (society), without agreements, appointments, or obligations. Nobody lived just in the moment, experiencing free will or as some say, free choice... in that state of being there isn't a must, only a may.

Born of Innocence, what did we know?

For most of us, just after birth, from the moment we open our eyes, we see the light of day. We are all equal perfect little beings, consisting of unconditional love. A great miracle! And then our journey begins, and believe we are visitors here and we forget that we are the miracles, and we are part of this existence.

Why are we born here?

We are born here to take care of this earth and its inhabitants, together with our fellow humans. For every one of us, there would be land and shelter, enough food, drinking water, free education, and free information. Seen from this perspective, this earth is a beautiful place where we can learn from each other by working together, build relationships based on friendship and even experience love. All based on free will. From a spiritual perspective, this life is also meant to solve problems, make up for quarrels, ultimately forgive ourselves and the other. If it is intended that way, then where did it go wrong, because most people really have to pay for everything and everyone.

If I look back on my life and I would describe my process it would look like this to me:

#didyouknow

Birth

You are born! Welcome to this existence, this is your
world.

How conception came about, the relationship of and
with your parents, culture, and situation in which you
grow up, is different for everyone. Our parents, who
also have no idea how to raise a child and usually have
not been given a perfect example from their parents,
try to make the best of it. They follow the rules that
have been imposed, for example, compulsory
education. This system works well, *as long as you
participate*. Immersed into the educational system, you
won't find out what's really going on. That's how
everyone starts, innocent, ignorant and often gullible.

Youth, our education.

Children attend school, spending 8 hours a day at
school, make friends, choose hobbies or sports and,
when they have fulfilled their serious tasks, they are
allowed free time to play outside, which is typically 30
minutes out of an 8-hour day. Children are trained to
view everything as a competition, such as perfecting
a musical performance or getting chosen to be on the
best side of a team in sports. This is how society
slowly trains, forms, and bends human beings, to fit
within a regimented society, following lines, class
rules, seeking permission from authority, mainly
working with very little playtime and exploration of
nature.

In reality, humans are prepared for something that increasingly stands outside ourselves and will force us to make moral choices that are not human. Conditioned and prepared for the 'real life' that is always ready and waiting for us to join – the workforce. The false competition of this 'real life' is the human burden and struggle for money and power, in which our society forces us to live by, getting caught in the peasant hamster wheel of low salary, high inflation, high taxes, and giving us a never-ending debt that we pay off with high interest. It is an endless cycle. Because of the great inequality and imbalance of the global elitist who run our society and the lower-class societies, we often find it financially and emotionally hard to survive. The government teaches us that we are the cause of all this, but that is one of their greatest lies. What is true, is that we continue to participate in it every day, forcing the competition to continue. Any way you look at it, this society's system always takes us one step further away from our true nature, from living a fulfilled and healthy life and being the best version of our-self.

As you can see, this story no longer fits with our original concept about why we are all here.

From an early age, what we are taught in school is determined by the authorities who manage the financial interests behind the scenes. We are forced to go to school without knowing that all our textbooks are carefully designed to prepare us for society's system that we will ultimately become a part of.

This society is completely based on agreements that enforce the notion that, 'time is money.' When in actuality, time is our most valuable energy. This means that we are imprisoned by mostly forced contracts, in exchange for our time they use up and consume our precious energy. With all of our energy consumed, we have little energy and time left for ourselves to wonder, imagine and use our creativity in creating a better, truer life for society; we simply stay stuck in the system as they intended.

When we work, we spend our money on things we need, which are created by large corporations, which increase inflation yearly, without increasing our salaries, which keeps us in the lower and middle income brackets of the population. These large corporations are backed by world globalists.

We are also forced to pay a substantial portion of our income in taxes to the government, again taking more money away from us. Not really trapped, but so limited that we can no longer choose what we really want to do or could do with our time because we need to make money to pay for the contracts. And the deeper we get into this society, most of us do not have the time to find out what we genuinely want to pursue in our lives or envision a different life.

Imagine spending your day exploring, learning, creating, and having fun with your time, finding a way to live a life of your dreams and make a career of it. When we are caught up on the hamster wheel of the 9-5 working cycle, we are unconscious, in constant fear of losing everything -- our shelter, bed, and food. This touches our emotions of shame and guilt, maybe more than the real fear of losing it all. But in this world where money talks, it exists for everyone who owns something. This fear also keeps society in the tension between money and power. Combined with the conditioned programming from early age, most people are often unaware, unconscious, or just having no idea and obey and follow authority, teachers, police officers, presidents, and their government.

All along, the government, the entire time has been in the background, setting this wheel in motion, making it look like they care about society, when in actuality, we are all enslaved to them– to work, buy their products, pay their taxes, making them more powerful and wealthy. We all fall victim to the government's coercion and corruption, until one day we become conscious, awake and aware and we try to detach ourselves from this society, or at best, find resolutions to make it better.

But no matter how we came to be, everyone eventually finds a way to provide for their living needs and maintenance or even to 'earn' money. We call this work, our way of how we are going to spend our time to earn money that pays the bills.

In exchange for your work in your time, you get paid money, which, you then have to hand over a gross amount to the government, in their form of products, housing, gas, insurance, liquor, medical, taxation, etc., which will only serve this system by you continuing to do so. This is all at the expense of the time that was inherently God given to you and owned by you, but you give it away in exchange for . . . well, what actually?

This is where you can start to put the pieces together and realize that you have been conditioned to go to school, obey authority, go to college, get a job, be a consumer and pay taxes. This is all designed mind control by the government to condition the entire society to stay within society's matrix.

We were all taught one way in school and rewarded and graded for the right answers, not thinking outside of the box. To support the concept of the government's mind control, the news and print media, social media, television, and film also fuels this system of control with the subconscious programming of our mind through direct or indirect subliminal messages. The news anchors and newspapers manipulated and provided scripts of what they are to inform the public on, which are all based on lies and instilling fear to keep us in the cycle and low vibrational.

To explain it a bit further for the laypeople among us, the newspaper gives people space to express their opinion about topics in the newspaper. The articles chosen by the newspaper is what is going on in the world. Through power structures, bosses or owners give the makers of the newspaper the right direction about what, according to their agenda is going on in the world. Also, the direction about which and how it is written in the articles, because the journalists and reporters who submit their stories are paid by the newspaper, so the newspaper chooses which stories we read. What the majority of people perceive and believe is going on among the population in the world is taken out of proportion, put into what they want us to know, read, hear, see, think and feel and then presented to us via, for example, the newspaper. The information they provide us is intended to keep us low vibrational, in a state of fear and enslaved in the matrix.

As, an older big brother of the newspaper there is television. This device literally broadcasts programs on the channel of your choice. The viewer does not realize that the program being watched also has another function. That is, the television device, programs the viewer and directs the predetermined storyline about what is going on in the world directly to your subconscious. This will slowly form your opinion. Nowadays the internet with the computer and our mobile phone has brought us more freedom of information, but even so, they are continuously censoring our information. They also do the same thing with the television when it comes to unconscious programming. Much of what I share here is information that is withheld, therefore not free and easily available, otherwise we all would have already known this, and we would no longer accept it. From an early age, we are therefore already unconsciously and without permission -- programmed by everything that comes to us via the media, telephones, and computers. Most information does not contribute to our well-being. Experts agree on that.

#didyouknow

Puberty, trying everything

During this period, you will become acquainted with
the things that come your way that will determine
your future life. You're going to find out what you like
and don't like, what is good or dangerous for you;
your moral grounds of good and bad will be tested,
but it is then up to you how you deal with this
yourself.

Here you will also make choices about the further
course of your life... which study, which friends, you
are introduced to, alcohol or drugs and sexuality.
Overall, a turbulent time.

Growing up, the role you play has to be more serious

You are prepared. At this time, most have found a job
or started their own business to provide for their lives.
This way you fit into society and this system. In this
role, you always serve your boss because that's what
you got hired for. That's how it was conceived, and
you participate. As an entrepreneur you have different
options but it's the same concept, there's little
freedom to break free, because there is no more real
free time as your mind is occupied with all this work.

But whatever career you choose, or how well your
business is running, eventually you find out that
material things do not bring happiness, and that
money does not really make you rich. It's all
temporary so you get back to what you're doing
without really thinking about what you're doing. And
more importantly, for what or for whom?

CHAPTER THREE

NOBODY IS IN
CHARGE

What are we doing here?

Let's assume you discover a new land and a new tribe
of people somewhere. From the first meeting they
were afraid of you and believed everything you told
them. They started working and building, anything
you asked them. If someone stood up, you took him
on your team and made him a leader of a project, or
you scared him so much that he disappeared.
Suppose this went on for hundreds of years, what
would become of that tribe? Now if we take this
example to the society we live in - a society where,
through all the corruption, good is ruled by evil.
Suppose we are the progeny of that new tribe that was
then discovered; then 'we' are the people who live
here, do our best to live a healthy life and try to make
the best of it.

On the other hand, seen through the eyes of the
rulers, our world to them is just one big laboratory,
where humans are just part of their experiment. The
controlled governments and secret projects are
poisoning us on all levels.

If we continue to obey in that experiment, as their
slaves, our behaviour will have a sad outcome for all
of humanity and for Mother Earth. This includes you
and me, as well as those in control and their followers
executing the orders.

Who are they and what is their role? This is where I
ask that you broaden your mind. '*They*' operate from a
shadow world and are called Archons. They are
hidden in another dimension. From there, using our
technology, such as computers, they test our brains,
just to experiment how far they can go with the
trauma-based mind control program. They use this
program to push fear-based agendas through the

propaganda networks, to make us participate in theirritual. That ritual is that we continue to do what we are told without thinking for ourselves, so slowly we go down together, staying low vibrational. The lower the vibration they keep us in, the harder it is for us to see the truth of what is going on. It sounds harsh but that's the reality. The way out is to wake up and see what's up; then you can start to make other choices.

The excuse, `I'm not ready`, or, `I'm too old for this nonsense`,
is precisely the plan of the elite rulers. As long as we don't believe what I am saying here is true,their matrixed society will go on as they intended.

Jamaican singer, musician and songwriter, Bob Marley long ago sang in the song, 'I Shot the Sheriff': *"Every day the bucket goes to the well, one day the bucket is full, and the bottom wil drop out".* That's where we all are. Our limits are always tested, in due time, at one moment it will be enough. When this moment arrives for all of humankind, it will create a kind of liberation that could resemble madness. Insanity is the light that breaks through the structures of belief so that control programs begin to fall apart, and you really see what is happening around you.

regarding Satanism:
The fall of men; which is the period of time where we are now.
Satanism, the oldest and hidden religion of the world, covers all levels of society. From Cultural Superstitious black magic religions to child sacrifice rituals. Freemason lodges are a coverup for this religion. I am uncertain if practitioners on various levels realize what they are sacrificing and that they are destroying themselves, as well as their energy, upholding a system that is designed to destroy humanity. Look at initiators and find out that new age and freemasonry are just cover names for satanism.

#didyouknow

CHAPTER FOUR

Nobody Explains their Lies

How are we manipulated?

Some people use the expression *'everything is a lie'*. I agree, if we simply look at our government that never takes responsibility, our corrupt justice system, all the negative news and violence in the mainstream media narrative. In short, they give us a kernel of truth inflated with lies. So, let's take a look at what that actually means, and how it affects our lives and therefore yours. So, to start at the beginning, what is a lie?

A lie is a statement that is believed to be false and is commonly used to mislead someone. This is seen from the one who spreads the lie. Seen from the receiver's point of view, you believe that what is stated is true and so you are thus misled.
The structure of a lie can be divided into two distinct types:
A lie can be a false description, a totally made-up story.

Or a lie can be a false denial. That is to deny that things have happened or have been said.

Cause - why do people lie?

The most common reason people use a lie is the urgent need to hide the truth. This creates division between people who believe it, and those who don't, with all its consequences. And that's exactly what the lie is for... to cause confusion.

Effect - what happens if we are lied to?

Lying makes us doubt our self-worth and creates a sense of guilt and unease in ourselves. We question a lie with, 'Why would they want to hurt us by lying; if they cared about me, they wouldn't lie to me'. As humans we believe in the concept that people are good, therefore if the government is in place for us, it must be there to do good for the people – when it is the opposite. The vast majority of people believe this concept, therefore, we continue to listen, trust and obey; forcing us to stay within the matrix. This can also drive people to frustration, anxiety, paranoia, sadness, and even clinical depression. This is perhaps the worst effect of lying, as it greatly hinders our selfimage and distorts the way we see and treat ourselves.

If we eventually lose faith in ourselves, the chances of continuing to use lies as our defence mechanism increase even more. Lying can also cause us to underestimate or overestimate other people and their abilities.

Why isn't the government telling us the truth honestly? The reason for this is that we are easier to control if we don't know the truth. Conversely, if we knew the truth of their agenda, we would stand up and no longer accept it. To go one step further, how does a lie serve authority?

If a question of truth goes unanswered, it has the same effect as a lie.

An example of an important unanswered question, *`Who controls this earth's society and its governments?`* None of us can answer this question because "they" don't want us to know who is controlling our society. Without this answer it is difficult to take responsibility for your own life, as there is no faith because you do not really know who to trust.

Looking deeper into the effects of a lie:

To give you an idea of how strong the lie can be when it is consciously conceived and shared, here is an example: *We slowly are being convinced that climate change is destroying the earth and it is our own fault. As a solution to the climate crisis, our government is putting contracts into place, instead of solving the problem with real solutions.* What would be their real agenda?

I agree that we should take care of our planet as a collective, but the means by which our planet is being destroyed are in the hands of the same global elites who are driving us to the climate crisis and then spinning it on us, that we are the cause of it. We have no choice but to vote for a political party to take action. To do something about this, we must position ourselves with the right to vote for a party that represents our voice to help as a country and society to protect the earth, save ourselves and leave something more beautiful for future generations. Our vote is therefore not used at all for our well-being. It gives us the illusion that by voting a politician in place that we have a voice. Politicians are voted into power, but have very little power, because they are ruled by the elites and actioned what to do. Now what is the secret power of the lies that rule us? *That it's all an illusion and the whole story is a lie.* Because there is no democracy in view of the public lies and mistakes. For example, politicians many times remain without consequences, while our choices have consequences, and we are held accountable. The plans for the agenda of our government are already in place, business has long been settled, as they continue to carry out their agenda. This is easy to research for yourself, as factual evidence for what I am a speaking

to. What is our role?
In the meantime, we are so caught up in the lie, we defend it because it is all we were ever taught to believe. We become busy proclaiming our opinion as the truth against our friends, acquaintances or somewhere on the internet and where necessary even defending it. In this way we unconsciously cooperate to maintain this whole story, which is not true in reality.

A deeper effect, if you choose to believe a lie *(for your convenience)*, you open yourself to the darkness of this world and invite the blindness of evil to take over your life; to the point where you can't even see the truth anymore and you go along with the crowd.

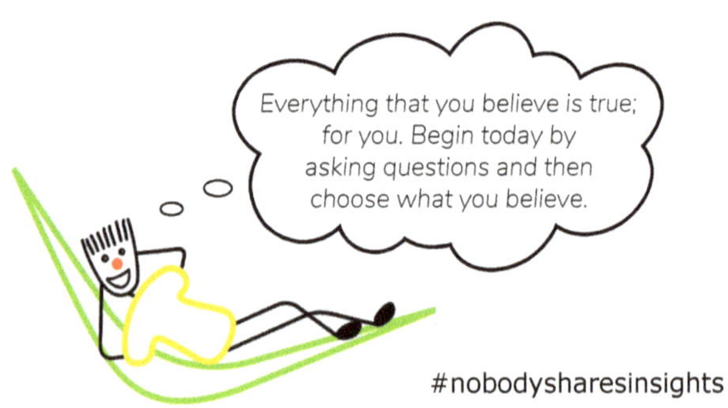

When will it stop? As long as you believe the lie, it will affect your life. Energetically you also give away your power, because your energy is in a low vibration, and with that, you become energetically lunch for the shadow entities that control us. They can enter your system through your mind if you are open to their lies. Simply explained, this is done through an energetic field, named Wetiko, which among other things, manipulates our emotions through other people and thus takes over our power. Once we give our power away, it uses our power against us, by projecting this back onto us in their lower vibration. That makes us stay in a low vibration, and they keep themselves and their existence intact. In short, we live in a delusional world and are food for shadow entities. But don't worry, it's nothing new what I'm telling you, but this is news that you should know right now to protect yourself against it or deal with it better; not to change the world, but to make your world a little better. So, let's move on…if everything is a lie, *what contracts do we have as humans?*

GOOD
BAD
This is GOOD!

CHAPTER FIVE

NOBODY IS FREE FROM CONTRACTS

How do they control us?

When you leave all your worldly possessions behind, you are free; this is called Moksha, easy to say, but not so easy to do, because we live in a world based on contracts and agreements. You can say that a contract is an official form of an agreement. The contracts you have entered into, are a commitment or obligation towards someone. This means that a person or company owns a part of your time or your energy, your energy is what you bring into this world. It is not easy for you to make your own choices with all the contracts you are already committed to. But there is a solution for everything. To understand this a little better, let's first take a look at what a contract actually is?

A contract is a legally enforceable agreement that creates, defines, and regulates the mutual rights and obligations between the parties.

Key elements for a valid contract:

1. Offer
2. Acceptance

Basic
Acceptance:

Your acceptance must reflect the offer; this means

1. In order to be valid and form a binding contract, the acceptance must correspond exactly
to the offer.
2. Acceptance must be communicated to the provider.

How does our government work? They come up with
all kinds of proposals that apply as laws and
regulations, preceded by a storyline in the media that
supports this. Then these laws... contracts for us, are
what we have to abide by without actually choosing to
do so. We are unaware of these contracts because they
are interwoven into the laws that make, forcing us to
abide by them.

Messages are posted through the media to give us the
idea that laws protect our safety, so that we believe we
need it and not rebel against the draconian measures
we regularly face. They then mix it all up and bring the
offers of contract by law, forcetheir government
mandates, force the media and marketing to carry out
propaganda supporting their narratives, and we have
no chance but to comply, or we break the law and face
fines and even imprisonment.

The most important notion they try to imply and
impose upon us, is our informed consent. They
assume that because we don't respond, that we give
our precious permission. What is consent or
acceptance?

Consent occurs when a person voluntarily agrees to
the proposal or wishes of another.

Informed consent is a principle in medical ethics and
medical law that a patient must have sufficient
information before making his own free decisions
about his medical care. The lack of clearly explained
information about the ingredients of the drug in
vaccination programs is a good example of this.

An example of reversed truth; in a natural

organic world, we should have informed consent for everything we consume; no fine print and E numbers, just clear labels with natural organic ingredients. In an ideal world, chemically toxic products would not be offered in any market. You can change this for yourself. You can ask a local farmer what he sells.

There are also many organic or bio stores where you can buy products with only organic ingredients, that are healthier for your body. Organic ingredients are often a little more expensive, but if you are a bit creative, you will discover that you can find almost all products in nature or grow them yourself in a small garden. It's also fun to do too.

Anyway, suppose this is one big experiment, they still need our full consent with anything they propose to us before we choose to contract. Without permission they harm me and every fellow human being on all levels.

To harm a human being is to violate the Natural Law. In order to establish this crime, one starts with a liability statement, *i.e., making the other person aware of his behaviour by officially holding him accountable in a letter*. This is a normal legal principle to indicate that you do not agree with something. It doesn't sound complicated, but the reality is different.

#didyouknow

As the collaborators of the secret agenda, working on both sides of the veil, public and hidden, infiltrating all levels of our society, this is the world we live in. The Archons, of which I will discuss in the next chapter, ruled our minds for a long time. This time has now come to an end. Why? Because the truth about the secret societies is known. As a result, their lies can no longer control us as humanity in its entirety. So, their time of total control is over and slowly but surely, they have to leave or may become extinct. As change approaches, we have to deal with what they left behind for us or, after years of destroying Mother Earth, *what's left of her.* The time has come when we as humanity, stand on our inner truth, our divine purpose and take action. This will turn the tables no matter where you live in the world. As a great collective, this inevitable event will heal our traumatised world of this false reality and bring nature back into balance.

When we awake and become conscious, we can clearly see that lobbyists and advisors run governments behind the scenes, out of the public eye, or in the shadows, as they call it. Our problem here is, our government rules our lives. To investigate some more, let's take a look at what 'shadows' really are and how you deal with them.

#nobodyslogic

CHAPTER SIX

NOBODY EXPLAINS
SHADOWS

Who are they?

Dear reader, in this chapter I will discuss how our shadow world, which we can normally not perceive, operates. This concept may seem overwhelming and may be a step too far for some. If you find this is the case, you can simply skip this chapter. If you read on however, you might find it to be very interesting.

#didyouknow

Let's talk about the Archons that operate and use the Wetiko field to control our mind and our emotions. The Wetiko field phenomena works against our natural response. So, when we are open to our emotions of fear, shame, guilt, hatred, regret, and pain, we 'voluntarily' feed them. Fear is their most common and preferred energy; sexual energy is their second favourite.

The Archon possessing entity can then drain the energy directly from the solar plexus of a human in this state.

The infection of such an Archon entity starts with lowering your vibration. This is achieved through addictive hooks, such as drugs, alcohol, porn, and pharmaceuticals, to name a few. If you associate with people of low character, distressed, or prone to anger/depression, you are at high risk of developing negative attachments to entities.
Addiction is highly susceptible, but not just to alcohol or drugs. Other forms of addiction can be, but are not limited to: masturbation, empty sexual relationships, pornography, abusing your partner, constantly judging others, gossiping, wishing for negative outcomes, food, thoughts of violence, material things, love of money and power, worshiping celebrities, pop or sports stars, gambling, and even having social media all affect your
well-being.

Who helps them?

In this world where we, "energetically" are the currency, they use money to control our time and they personally control our minds, as explained above. That's how they direct us and that's how we create this collective memory and thus one can state that we create it ourselves. We will now discuss the question, *'What about our free will ?'*

Those in power on earth serve their agenda. Some would say that these power-hungry controllers are Reptiles/Greys. This is the role they must play. They are completely possessed and have no free will anymore. They just live an archonic agenda and put us in an energetic prison to become food. We have been under their influence and their property for thousands of years. Satanism keeps this secret hidden and serves the Demiurge, the same leader as that of the Archons. You can see Satanism as a faith for them, where this world and the world we have to live in are brought together. The choice in free will is often forgotten or ignored, while this is precisely *our strength.* If many people say no, something will change.

Basically, they control our creation, which is our life, and they operate from the shadows. This looks like an illusion, a system created and pulled over our eyes, and that made us pay for everything. They also made up laws and lies to make us play roles and conform to the choices they wanted us to make. It's not that complicated for them as they understand our ego better than we do. Let's see how we can deal with this hidden enemy of humanity and understand how these shadows act and operate so you can recognize them in your own life.

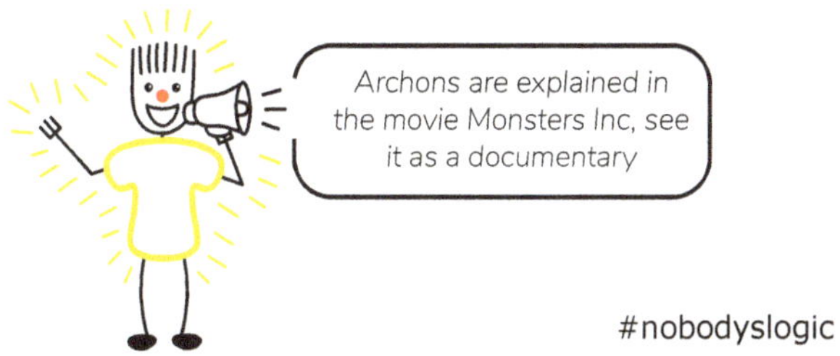

#nobodyslogic

CHAPTER SEVEN

NOBODY HANDLES HANDLERS

How do they operate?

With or without our knowledge we are the controllers or supervisors, or we are checked and supervised. In our last chapter, I talked about shadows and how they control us. Now we are going to explain this in our human world. The intermediaries who ensure that the tasks are carried out properly is a handler. What does that actually mean?

Handler - A person or thing that acts.

- A routine that controls communication with, or control of, an external unit.

(literally) Someone who handles something (especially manually) or someone.

(in combination) A controller, trainer, someone who guides a particular person.

For example, a person employed by a record company to advise a celebrity on what to say or do, such as when shaping his or her public image, is a public handler. American singer, songwriter, dancer and actress, Britney Spears had a lot of problems with her handler.

Now let's take a closer look at our own world, with the people, friends, and family we are surrounded with.
Unhealthy relationships exist at all levels, from a disturbed family relationship, to a power struggle with your manager, an overzealous police officer on the street, or just that awful neighbour who always has to say something to ruin the mood. This is often narcissistic behaviour, based on (childhood) trauma.

So, when this is done intentionally, for their own benefit by people with a narcissistic personality, the victims are subjected to psychological torture every time and they often also have to deal with the so-called Stockholm Syndrome. The Stockholm Syndrome, which creates sympathy for the perpetrator, gives you a feeling of guilt that prevents you from thinking and acting clearly. For example, the power game is interwoven in society, and we are therefore led and guided by several people every day.

If the victim never gets out of this role, he will always be controlled or treated by the doer who is not really a perpetrator but actually also a victim – the classic empath/narcist relationship.

We must keep in mind that the narcissist has a Narcissistic personality disorder — one of several types of personality disorders — which is a mental condition in which people have an inflated sense of their own importance, a deep need for excessive attention and admiration, troubled relationships, and lack of empathy for others. The development of narcissistic trai is in many cases, a consequence of neglect or excessive apprais

On a personal level we all have handlers who advise or guide us. We also do this ourselves with others, for example when our advice or point of view is requested.

Seen from good intentions, it is to share knowledge to help someone further, or to grow in life. With bad intentions, it can be used to hide the outcome of past wrongs or to serve a secret agenda in a larger plan. It all seems far from our beliefs, but because it happens via guiding thoughts or energetically, we have to deal with it consciously or unconsciously on a daily basis. The denial doesn't make it go away.

Knowledge is power in this.

In the bigger picture, the Archons are responsible and keep us, as an unconsciously hypnotized society, in a low vibration by feeding us fear propaganda. This keeps us doing what they want us to do, and I explained that earlier in the chapter discussing lies. As soon as we see this, a change begins in ourselves. When we collectively get to the point where we stop giving away our power by believing that the matrixed society is all true, their entire show is over.

Stop denying yourself!

That's how it works folks, for spiritual teachers and healers who haven't started healing themselves, as any teacher should tell the students after initiation. Then they're in that passive, neutral mindset of not wanting to face reality because they're afraid to face themselves. If you don't own yourself, something else will come in your name that will take ownership of you and use yourself against you. And you won't even know it because you're denying yourself.

#didyouknow

CHAPTER EIGHT

NOBODY DIVIDES REALITY

Life is all about intention

In our world, I make a distinction and use the words; satanic and divine. Like two different sides of the same coin. This can help you see that everyone here, including you, has a choice from your intent and thus can choose which reality you want to live in or which creation you want to give your energy to.

Use your Intution

It is important for you to start questioning everything around you, what is being taught to you, what the news is telling on television and through social media. Question every social media post, even Time, Forbes, CDC, WHO - if they all match the same narrative as the news, you can bet they are being fed this news by the powers that be to keep you tied into the lies, the illusion. Think critically for yourself. Use your intuition to guide you. Your intuition will come to you in ways that are subtle or not so subtle. Your intuition might be telling you that (i) something doesn't feel right about this; (ii) you will have a gut feeling; (iii) you'll feel it in your bones; (iv) you have a sense that something is off; or (v) you'll get chills. This is your intuition, which is your higher self, guiding you – alerting you to pay attention, ask questions, dig deeper to find the truth.

satanic	divine
I am	I am
hate is the basis	love is the basis
lies	truth
mind-control (ego)	heart energy (beyond the ego)
use manipulation for control	here to celebrate life
hate 'useless' people	love human relationships
use low vibration symbols	use high vibration symbols
rituals to connect with death	rituals to celebrate life
nothing is sacred	everything is sacred
here to serve oneself	here to serve others
do what you will	thy will be done

CHAPTER NINE

NOBODY PLAYS BY THE RULES

How to deal with them?

Everything is energy. Communication is the giving, receiving, and sharing of information. It is important to know the 'art of conversation' as we connect with others during a conversation. Information shared in communication can be distributed in three different ways:

(i) 7% consists of spoken words, (ii) 55% of the information comes through body language, and (iii) 38% through the
tone of your voice.

Comunication explained in energy

Conversation is communication between people.

A conversation starts with a question, followed by an answer. After the question has been answered in an equal conversation, the other party can ask a question; once this is answered it will start again. If one breaks through this and asks more questions or answers your question with a question, there is a reason for it. By delving deeper into the subject at that time or at a better time, you will find out whether this person is more interested in your energy or really in you as a friend. As a true friend, a conversation should continue.

#didyouknow

It is therefore wise to learn to deal with this, so that, for example, you do not carry the (negative) thoughts of others with you after a conversation.

On the other hand, a conversation is a perfect instrument to bring energetic equality between all participants. Knowing the rules and using them as etiquette in conversation is a sign of authority.

Nobody likes to play by the rules and ask questions that confirm what the other has said. Once the question is confirmed there is a fair ground or connection, and from there the conversation goes in a certain direction. Simply asking a question about the truth that has been proclaimed, just to see if what has been said is true, which changes all the dynamics, and you can then tell what the other person's true intent is.

Who is Asking, is As King!

Then at least you have status. Since authority all works, acts, and behaves in a way called implicit consent, they will behave in a way that suggests you have all consented. And unless you deny that permission, unless you stop doing that, unless you say, wait a minute, I'm not giving permission, and I'm not agreeing to it. I am not a name, I appeal to common law; if you want to contract, I would be happy to work with you. My rate is 900 euros for an hour. Do we have a contract, yes or no?

source: Alan of Salisbury

#didyouknow

NOBODY SPEAKS TRUTH

Walk the talk

Many years ago, during my period of madness or
Satori as they call it in India, I was there at a local,
more or less underground party on the island of Ibiza.
I looked at all the people there and thought for
myself,
*Here we are in Ibiza, a spiritual university in this world, with
all these wonderful people, who consciously or forced, choose
to walk away from the system or society, to start, anew, to
be a different or better version of themselves.* Frankly, I
was not impressed. What I didn't see then, I know
now and see clearly. These people were consumed by
alcohol and drugs, they were lost souls, possessed by
shadows, dressed as people. They pretended.

The truth about people who pretend, they lie to
themselves. But why? Isn't it the truth that will
set us free? The reason is that we all live in mass
hypnosis through mind control.

Wetiko

To keep you informed, the field that feeds on these low vibrational frequencies is called Wetiko. You can say it bothers us as humans, and then use the reaction it causes against us. It takes away our life energy. Without knowing how it works, it is inescapable because of the dynamics of Wetiko in our own energetic field. Viewed from a positive perspective, this is the tool that the universe or divine creator uses to test our brains and moral grounds, just to find out who is strong enough to escape this mind and connect with the heart vibration

source: Paul Levy.

What to do or how to deal with this to get started? Take time for yourself in nature; a few times a week or if you can, twenty minutes every day will help you a lot. When you go out into nature, make sure you go without a phone, sitting quietly and doing nothing, looking around or writing something. With this.

#didyouknow

Stop doing things you don't want to do. Clear communication is central to this. The effect is that you stop playing the roles that no longer serve your well-being. The result is that you are more honest with yourself, have room to make new choices and slowly but surely start to feel better.

Everything divinely happens at the right time. Therefore, when everything is meant to be, all you need to do is surrender to trust. When you get into a situation where someone else is breaking your boundaries, and if you feel strong in that moment, this is *'your time to act wisely'* and serve yourself and therefore humanity. How? By *trusting your intuition, standing on your moral ground, and asking why?* With honest intentions, you begin to ask for the true reason of the other's behavior. The sometimes-painful answers can liberate you because you learn something, and you begin to realize that you can solve it for yourself. It can also bring some sort of justice simply by bringing the truth to the surface. So, staying calm and just keep asking why, will break all manipulation techniques and put you back in control of your life. If you master the technique of questioning, the result is that you have total control over the situation, and you feel this inner power. By practicing using your intuition, standing your moral ground, and not blindly following the matrixed society, you will raise your vibration to its highest intended form. Just imagine how this works once people recognize the vibration in themselves and others and want the same. With all of humanity at their highest vibration, we break their system. Just imagine this powerful high vibration of love all at once with the entire collective on Earth. This is love of humanity, in full force!

Now let's go back to the beginning, if this life is a big game, how does it end? As with all games, at some point in time, it comes to an end because there is a winner or because the other players no longer want to participate or play the game. That's when it's over.

Then all roles and rules of the game stop and we continue with the order of the day. The pawns and the game board go back into the box and are stored. All the players are equal again. In the end, it was never about winning, it was about participating, learning life's lessons, taking back your divine power and your God given sovereignty. I hope that when it's over you can look back on this interesting but beautiful period with confidence and be proud of yourself for your participation in changing society for the greatest good of humanity and our divine purpose on Earth.

You did it anyway!

"TRY THIS AT HOME"

To close this educational booklet,
I leave you with 2 challenging suggestions
to get out of the comfort zone and
make your world a better place:

"Act of kindness"

We can only transcend the Ego through service.
Play the good intention game.
Do something positive for someone else, just for fun.

"One day without..."

Challenge your boundaries.
Live one day without:
i.e., coffee, smoking, telephone, shoes,sleep; think
of something that you indulge in that you can go
without for one day.

Thank you!

I would like to thank everyone who supported me in this
process. A special thank you for giving more
clarity about the direction of my writing for Tess,
Aubrey , Sahifa and Wouter.

I wrote this story out of love for my children

Nobody knows how loved you are

Testing Testing; have a laugh with yourself.

Stand in front of a mirror now
look at your eyes
and say out loud:
"Nobody loves me!"
and see what happens...

For the brave among us, here it goes:

'AN ACT OF KINDNESS'

Start a local movement yourself or with friends and bring
a smile to your world!

Play the role of 'Nobody'
What you'll need: a yellow T-shirt red clowns nose

What you got to do:

Dress up, go sit somewhere among other people and:

- Practice the art of doing nothing. or

- Interview others about fun things in their lives.

or just ask someone new in the group:

How can I help?

Life is about giving and receiving.
An act of kindness or a good deed of kindness
has been long forgotten.

Being a 'nobody' for a moment is enough to change the
atmosphere in whatever situation you find yourself in.

it brings a smile to
the people around you.
I-)

WOOHOO NOBODY IS BORN!

If you want to know how this beautiful baby grows up and is going to move in this world, then take a look at our website.

Maybe you'll see something funny that resonates with you.

Blog and Vlog where admirers of this story can share something:
Nobody want to be Famous where others can post fun photos or short videos to compete for the

"Nobody of the Year Award!"

We develop ideas like:

Nobody is an Act of Kindness

Blog where stories of others can be posted.
and of course, an important question that Nobody asks...

Who is Ms. Nobody?

Also recording podcasts with fun themes like:
-        Nobody talks to themselves
-        Nobody is Live & Direct
-        Nobody meets ...

just visit us or become a member of the society
www.nobodyisdivine.com

From the perspective of
Happiness is sharing`
if this book was gifted to you
or you got it for free,
please do me a little favour
to get some things moving.

Find Mr. Nobody and leave your review on
Amazon
https://www.amazon.com/~/e/B0B5YNV1ZR

we are also to be found on
Apple Books, Google Play and many more

Definition Page

Archon =
In Gnosticism, the archons (from Greek arkhon, "ruler"[1]) were malevolent, sadistic beings who controlled the earth, as well as many of the thoughts, feelings, and actions of humans. They assisted their master, the demiurge, with the creation of the world, and continued to help him administer his oppressive rule.

Demiurge =
In the Platonic school of philosophy, the Demiurge is a deity who fashions the physical world in the light of eternal ideas. In the Timaeus, Plato credits the Demiurge with taking preexisting materials of chaos and arranging them in accordance with the models of eternal forms.

Ego =
Ego is a person's sense of self-esteem or self-importance. Ego is the part of the mind that mediates between the conscious and the unconscious and is responsible for reality testing and a sense of personal identity.

Moksha =
Moksha, also called vimoksha, vimukti and mukti, is a term in Hinduism, Buddhism, Jainism and Sikhism for various forms of emancipation, enlightenment, liberation, and release.

Natural Law =
Natural law is a system of law based on a close observation of human nature, and based on values intrinsic to human nature that can be deduced and applied independently of positive law.

Reptiles/Greys =
Some UFO experts believe that Grey aliens were a slave race created by the powerful Draco Reptilians. The purpose

for the Greys was to harvest the "negative energy" of other races. It is reported that the Greys revolted however and formed certain pacts with human governments. The Greys are a suppose dying race and need humans to continue their hybrid program to extend the life of their race.

Satori =
Satori means the experience of awakening ("enlightenment") or apprehension of the true nature of reality.

Solar plexus =
The solar plexus — also called the celiac plexus — is a complex system of radiating nerves and ganglia. It's found in the pit of the stomach in front of the aorta. It's part of the sympathetic nervous system. It plays a significant role an important role in the functioning of the stomach, kidneys, liver, and adrenal glands.

Stockholm Syndrome =
Stockholm syndrome is a coping mechanism to a captive or abusive situation. People develop positive feelings toward their captors or abusers over time. This condition applies to situations including child abuse, coach-athlete abuse, relationship abuse and sex trafficking.

Wetiko =
In its Native American meaning, wetiko is an evil cannibalistic spirit that can take over people's minds, leading to selfishness, insatiable greed, and consumption as an end in itself, destructively turning our intrinsic creative genius against our own humanity.

About the author

How am I doing with my life?

I am seen as a human with a spiritual experience

I am here to experience free will. I know that I am a child of the Creator, learning how to use my sovereign status and live my highest potential. As a human being, nothing or no-one owns me. I have no obligations, no debts, and no contracts against my will.